Come and Hug Me

Michal Snunit

Illustrated by
Vanessa Levy

Translated by
Yael Lotan

Robinson
LONDON

When the sky was born
so was the earth,
when the plants were born
so were the animals.
When the people were born
with them came

THE LANGUAGE OF THE HUG

**The language of the hug
is the oldest language of all.**

It was born even before the words.

**It has its own SIGNS
which everyone
learns to recognize very quickly.**

When we are born, Mother takes us
in her arms, very gently,
so as not to startle us, and gives us
a hug.
From this hug the milk begins to
flow to us
from Mother's body.
Our first food
starts with a hug which is WARM
and sweet.

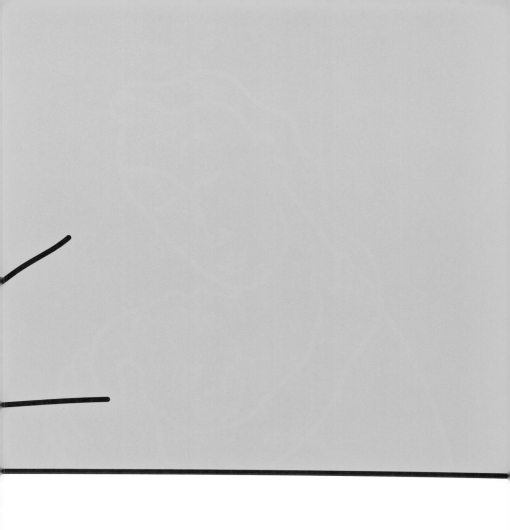

Is that how the earth feels
when the sky touches and hugs it
in the long fine line we call
the horizon?

When the sky was born
so was the earth,
when the plants were born
so were the animals.
When the people were born
with them came
the language of the hug.

In this language every hug is different. And just as you can tell plant from plant, animal from animal,
person from person, so too you can tell one hug from another.

The hug of flower and butterfly is
sweet as nectar –
a quick light hug.
The flower stands still, waiting
for the butterfly to come and hug it.
The butterfly hovers over the flower,
touches its petals and flies on.
ONE FLOWER IS NOT ENOUGH
FOR IT.
Its life is short and many are the
flowers.

The hug of tree and bird.
What song does the bird sing to the
tree?
What does it whisper to the leaves?
When evening falls the tree hugs
the bird,
keeping it warm in the chill air.
All through the night they sleep
hugging each other,

sharing a dream.

When the sun shines
The bird spreads its wings.
It flies into the arms of heaven
bringing greetings
with its hug.

The mountain hugs the rock.

The river hugs the fish.

The cloud hugs the rainbow.

Therefore the rock does not fall,
the fish can live,
and the rainbow paints the world
in colours of honey and milk.

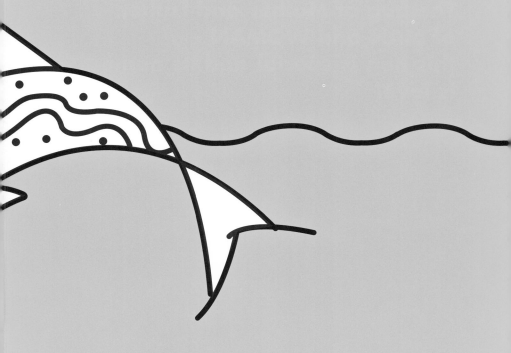

Those who hug under the sky
can see the radiance of the stars,
which cherish and guard
all truly loving couples.

The hug of Eve and Adam –
The two who were the parents of
all who live on earth.

The hug of Mother and Father,
of MAN and WOMAN –
this hug is special and its name
is love.

After the sky was born,
and the earth,
after the plants were born
and the animals,
people were born and with them
was also born
the language of the hug,

whose sign is LOVE.

And if ever you have loved
and you still feel love,
you know that it's a JOY –

but has some pain in it.

For it takes two to hug.
It is not possible to HUG alone.

**Whom will the tree hug,
unless it has a bird?**

**Whom will the mountain hug,
unless it has a rock?**

**Whom will the river hug,
unless it has a fish?**

**The flower waits for the butterfly
to come and touch its petals.**

And people have a great
language of hugs.
There is NO END to what
a hug can do.

For instance,
Some like to hug each other
all over, body to body.

Others like to hug each other lightly
with their fingertips.

Some people hug without a touch,
ONLY WITH THEIR EYES.
Their hugs are hardly seen
by others.

Then there are **HUGE** hugs,
that reach up to the sky.
And hugs that come up from the feet.
In some hugs the hands go wild.
There are laughing hugs,
and cheer-up hugs
to drive out loneliness.
And hugs of gladness,
and also hugs of fear
that we must part.

A hug of peace after a row
is very gentle, never hurts.

Light touches darkness,
night seeks day.
Those are the hugs of opposites.

A hug with a dance.
A hug within a hug.
And suddenly a farewell hug.

A gentle hug to say "Good night".
A special one that says "Hello",
and one that only says "Goodbye".

**Then there's a hug of LONG AGO,
a wistful one,
deep in the heart
never to be forgotten.**

There are no words
in the language of the hug,
nor are there empty hugs.
And what we hope for above all –

is for our hug to go on for ever.

Robinson Publishing Ltd
7 Kensington Church Court
London
W8 4SP

This edition first published
in the UK by Robinson
Publishing Ltd 1999

The moral right of the
author has been asserted.

10 9 8 7 6 5 4 3 2 1

A copy of the British
Library Cataloguing in
Publication data is
available from the
British Library.

ISBN 1–84119–044–6

Printed and bound in the EC